CONTENTS

CHAPTERS

ACTIVITIES

ACKNOWLEDGEMENTS

The workbook would not be here without the stalwart efforts of a number of people – we'd like to thank them here.
For knocking us and our ideas into shape, we would like to thank Shelagh Smith, Simon Shellard, Aidan Tod, Jacqui Hartas,
Ruth Robertson, Paul Fairhurst, Mike Pegg, Nicki Hayes and Nigel Minton. And for their great work on the look and feel of the
workbook, a shout goes out to Clive Oakes, Anna Barley, Tamsin Pickeral and Odette Beris. Finally, thanks to everyone who has
inspired us along the way – you know who you are.

James and Paul, September 2010.

ABOUT THE AUTHORS

Dr Paul Brewerton, BA (Hons), MA, MSc, PhD, Chartered Occupational Psychologist

Paul is Co-Founder and Director of Strengths Partnership Ltd, a specialist provider of strengths-focused assessment and training services.

A Chartered Occupational Psychologist with 15 years experience in leading successful consulting practices and projects, Paul is passionate about helping organisations to achieve success through their people using the practical application of psychological tools and techniques.

Over the past few years Paul has increasingly focused on the practical application of strengths and positive psychology to organisations, assisting them in developing positive, productive cultures.

Paul has worked with a diverse range of clients including the Natural History Museum, Bank of England, Police Service of Northern Ireland, Royal Air Force, Learning and Skills Council, Abbey, Takeda, Oracle, Panasonic and many other organisations.

James Brook, Masters in Organisational Psychology, MBA, FCIPD

James is Co-Founder and Director of Strengths Partnership Ltd, a specialist provider of strengths-focused assessment and training services.

An accomplished Executive Coach, Facilitator, Consultant and Speaker, he has over 15 years experience developing high performing leaders, teams and organisations through helping people optimise their distinctive strengths and competencies.

James has strong international experience and has run consulting, training and coaching projects for a variety of organisations including Allen and Overy, CareerBuilder, Foster Wheeler, ING Direct, Kellogg, Brown and Root, Novartis Pharmaceuticals, Tesco, Shell and Yahoo!

James has a Masters Degree in Industrial & Organisational Psychology and an MBA from the University of Maryland in the U.S.A., as well as an Advanced Diploma in Executive Coaching. He is a Fellow of the Chartered Institute of Personnel and Development (FCIPD), and is also a member of the Association of Business Psychologists.

FOREWORD

Congratulations on having taken the first steps on your strengths journey. Becoming more aware of your strengths, however, is just the start.

In order to translate your strengths into personal and business success, you will need to invest time, effort and energy in improving your work habits and capitalising on your strengths. Through following the simple techniques and 4-A Strengths to Success development process in this workbook, you will gain:

- AWARENESS of your strengths (what energises you and keeps you going)
- ACTION (or the inspiration you need to take action to use and develop your strengths and reduce limiting weaknesses)
- AGILITY (or the ability to use your strengths in an agile, balanced way)
- ACHIEVEMENT (Building and reinforcing cycles of success and recognising your achievements)

> "Your time is limited, so don't waste it living someone else's life ...have the courage to follow your heart and intuition"
>
> Steve Jobs, CEO Apple, C21st

Please turn the page to find out more about each stage of the process.

4 STEPS TO SUCCESS THROUGH MAKING YOUR STRENGTHS PRODUCTIVE

1. Build a good AWARENESS of your strengths

Most people understand their weaknesses far better than their strengths, yet it is your natural strengths (or *personal qualities that make you feel energised and lead to peak performance*) that are sources of mastery and success at work. Your strengths also enable you to deal with challenging and stressful times with greater confidence and resilience.

To achieve excellence, you need a good understanding of your strengths and how to match these with the organisation's goals to ensure your contribution is focused on activities that are most important to your business.

2. Take ACTION to optimise strengths and reduce limiting weaknesses

Optimise standout strengths

Strengths-building is hard work, requiring careful planning to develop the skills, knowledge and productive habits to get the most from your strengths. However, you will also need to execute your plan with determination and discipline, bringing in different people to support, coach and guide you along the way. There is simply no substitute for deliberate practice so find *stretch* opportunities at work and outside to continuously fine-tune your strengths.

Reduce limiting weaknesses

To achieve sustained peak performance, you can't ignore weaknesses. If you do, this may result in low self-confidence, performance problems and even failure. However, not all weaknesses are equally important. Ensure you pinpoint weaknesses that limit your job performance and future success.

Put in place specific actions to improve these areas to at least a basic level of competence which is required in the job. A good place to start is to see whether any of your standout strengths can compensate for, or help you reduce your limiting weaknesses. Bringing in others to complement you in areas where you have weaknesses is also a great way to make weaknesses less relevant.

3. Strive to be AGILE in the way you use your strengths

Peak performers learn how to get the most from their strengths regardless of the situation. They are agile and adapt themselves to the environment with speed and precision.

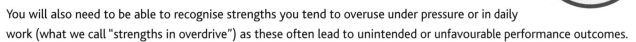

In order to build agility, it is necessary to move outside your "zone of comfort" to learn how to apply your strengths, skills and knowledge in unfamiliar work situations.

You will also need to be able to recognise strengths you tend to overuse under pressure or in daily work (what we call "strengths in overdrive") as these often lead to unintended or unfavourable performance outcomes.

By using the right strength (or strength combinations) at the right time and in the right amount, you will achieve success regardless of what is thrown your way.

4. Celebrate ACHIEVEMENT and build momentum for future success

Many of us tend to take our achievements for granted and don't take time to enjoy what we have achieved or learned from successes as well as shortfalls.

Look for what's working well and find meaningful ways to recognise and celebrate your strengths and achievements. This will help you build inner strength, self belief and resourcefulness for future success.

Maintain momentum for change by choosing an accountable, solutions-focused attitude, learning from successes and failures, inviting feedback and looking for further stretch opportunities.

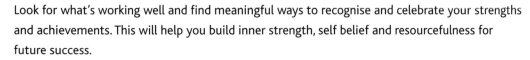

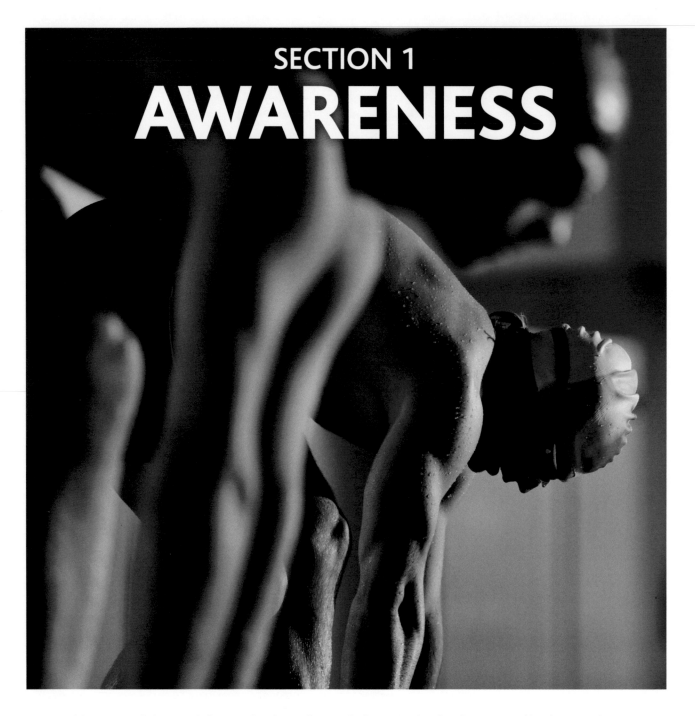

SECTION 1
AWARENESS

A strength is a personal characteristic or quality that makes you feel energised and enthusiastic and leads to you doing great work. Becoming fully aware of your strengths is the first step towards putting them to good use. This section helps you to do just that.

CHAPTER 1.1 – FINDING YOUR STRENGTHS

By now, you will have reflected on what your Strengthscope™ Feedback Report tells you about yourself. Soon you will drill down into your *Significant 7* and clarify your *Top 3 Strengths*. First though, it's worth tuning into your past. Why? Because in order to do more of what we do best, we need to gain a deep understanding of our positive patterns. Great though the Strengthscope™ analytic tool is, there's nothing like interrogating our past to ensure that what it is telling us is true.

So:

- Put the Strengthscope™ Feedback Report to one side
- Make sure you will not be disturbed for the next 20 minutes
- Make yourself a cup of your favourite brew
- Take a few deep breaths – or do whatever helps you let go of the thoughts that are racing in your mind...

You are going to interrogate your past.

You are going to become fully aware of your productive habits.

You are going to prepare yourself for your positive future...

> "Hide not your talents, they for use were made. What's a sundial in the shade?"
>
> Benjamin Franklin, C18th

Activity 1 – My Positive Pattern

Without reference to your Strengthscope™ Feedback Report, please complete the following sentences:

The three words which describe me at my best are:

The specific achievements that have been the most positive and memorable for me in my life (work, family, social) are:

These are important to me because:

A recent (ideally in the past six months) high point for me at work was:

This is what I did right; these are the results and this is what I learnt about myself:

CHAPTER 1.2 – FINDING YOUR FLOW

Remember the Strengthscope™ definition of a strength?

"A personal characteristic or quality that makes you feel energised and enthusiastic and leads to you doing great work."

Well, the *"makes you feel energised"* bit gives us another clue as to what your strengths may be. The following activities will help you to focus in on where you are in *flow*[1], identifying what it is that gives you energy, and what takes it away. Becoming aware of these energy fillers and drillers will help you when it comes to Section 2 of this workbook – putting your strengths into action.

Activity 2 – My Energy Lifeline

What gives you energy and what takes it away?

On the next page, please draw two lines to represent your energy levels in each of these areas of your life up to this point:

- Family/Home – immediate and extended family and home life
- Education/Work – your work and career experiences

For each area:

1   Think about when you felt most positive and energetic, representing these occasions by drawing your lifeline **above** the *zero* line on the graph.

2   Think about times when you felt drained and run down, representing these occasions by drawing your lifeline **below** the zero line.

3   You may also want to write key events on the graph, e.g. schooldays, birthdays, leaving college/university, meeting partners, successes at work, memorable holidays, etc.

4   You may even want to include your age or dates at the bottom of the graph, from the date of your birth, up to now.

5   Try to focus on how energised you felt at each point in your life as you draw the lifeline.

6   You may want to use a different colour for each area, or even to refer back to Activity 1 to help you focus.

---

[1] *Flow* is a concept that is explained in more detail in Chapter 2.4. It refers to a state of optimal performance, where the person is fully immersed in what s/he is doing, often referred to as *being in the zone*.

Now

Positive/energised

Negative/drained

Birth

Education/work

Family/home

Energy Levels

Activity 3 – My Fillers & Drillers

From your energy lifeline, and your reflections before the activity, what conclusions can you draw about what *fills* you the most with energy in work and in life, and what *drills* holes in your energy reserves in work and in life? What *gives* you energy and what *takes* your energy away?

My energy fillers at work are:

My energy drillers at work are:

My energy fillers at home are:

My energy drillers at home are:

What do your answers to the above tell you about your strengths (remember, strengths are personal characteristics or qualities that **make you feel** energised and enthusiastic and lead to you doing good work)?

TOP TIP

Sometimes these energy *drillers* and *fillers* can be activities (or types of activities – e.g. for people with *collaboration* as a strength, working in groups may be a *filler*; for those with *decisiveness* as a strength, consulting widely before making decisions may be a *driller*). Sometimes they can be people (or types of people, e.g. for those with *common sense* as a strength, when other people play their *creativity* strength in overdrive, this may become a driller, and vice versa).

CHAPTER 1.3 – YOUR *SIGNIFICANT 7*

OK. So you've finished the personal interrogation of your past, for now at least. Hopefully it has given you further insight into your unique set of strengths. Now it is time to pick up your Strengthscope™ Feedback Report again. Let's see how it compares to your notes. Let's drill down into your *Significant 7* (your seven highest ranked strengths when compared with the general working population).

Turn to Section 2 of your Strengthscope™ Feedback Report and look through the strengths that appear there. Read the definitions for each strength and look at the pictures too (they have been selected to appeal to people with those particular strengths).

Remember that a strength is an underlying quality or personality characteristic that energises you and makes you feel *stronger* when you use it at work or elsewhere. It is not a skill or competence.

While your *Significant 7 Strengths* are your highest, you are likely to also have other strengths which haven't quite made it into the list but which remain particularly important and energising to you. The exercises you have just completed may have helped to bring these to light.

It's time to find out more...

Activity 4 – My *Significant 7*

Referring to your *Significant 7*, as identified in Section 2 of your Strengthscope™ Feedback Report, please complete the following sentences:

These strengths from my *Significant 7* 'jump out' as being most true or descriptive of me; they provide me with the greatest source of energy at work:

These *Significant 7* Strengths surprise me; they surprise me because:

Your *Standout Strengths*

Often it is obvious which strengths are your greatest because they are the ones that give you the most energy. Energy begets energy so focusing in on your standout strengths gives you the greatest chance of releasing your true potential at work. It's not that your remaining strengths are less important. It's simply a case of prioritising areas for focus early on so that you can enjoy some quick wins whilst you consider how to build on and develop your strengths further.

At this stage, most people are beginning to see a pattern. Typically, between two and four of their *Significant 7 Strengths* stick out and their answers to activities 1 – 3 above reflect these *standout strengths*. Identifying those strengths that best describe you and communicating in your own words what you feel like and what happens when you use them, is the next step in raising your awareness of your personal strengths.

Activity 5 – My Top 3 Strengths

Based on your Strengthscope™ Feedback Report and mindful that your descriptions will be unique – as no one will have experienced using your strengths in quite the same way you have - please complete the following sentences:

My first *standout strength* at work, described in my own words, is:

This is one example of how I have used it, and how it made me feel:

My second *standout strength* at work, described in my own words, is:

This is one example of how I have used it, and how it made me feel:

My third *standout strength* at work, described in my own words, is:

This is one example of how I have used it, and how it made me feel:

How Productive are Your Strengths?

In order for your strengths to be productive, they need to be combined with relevant knowledge and skills and used in a way that brings value to your organisation. So, strengths should help the business achieve its goals in some way in order to be useful and relevant.

For example, if one of your standout strengths is *strategic mindedness*, but you haven't yet had the chance to gain knowledge and skills associated with the strength, then you may not be in the best position to help your organisation benefit from this strength. It may well remain hidden or under-used, so providing little value to you and your organisation. The exercise below should help you to work out how your *standout strengths* can be put to best use by using the skills and knowledge you have to optimise your strengths.

Activity 6 – Optimised vs. Sub-optimised Strengths

Using the diagram below, identify the 3 most important skills and knowledge areas you bring to your role together with your 3 *standout strengths* identified in Activity 5.

Next, identify the *productive habits* or successful patterns of behaviour you have which enable you to translate these qualities into successful outcomes at work.

For example, you may have a *decisiveness* standout strength, a skill in building rapport with customers and a deep knowledge about a particular product area in your organisation. Your productive habit may be that you can quickly get customers to make a decision on which product they want and make their purchase.

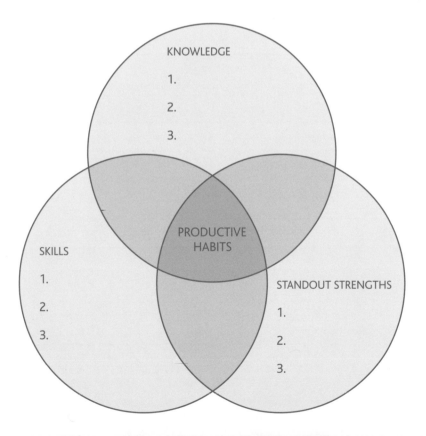

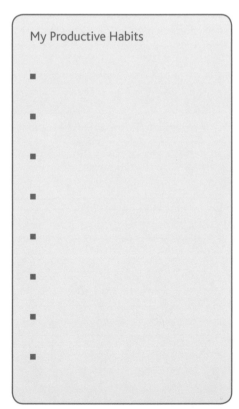

Having completed the diagram, you may find that some of your strengths are really well served by your knowledge and skills, as you have developed productive habits that get the most from these strengths.

For some other strengths, it may be that your knowledge and/or skills could be further improved to give you the best chance of developing productive habits.

Take some time to reflect on your completed diagram by answering the questions below.

The productive habits that are most important for me to accomplish my goals are:

The productive habits that are most well developed are:

Skills and knowledge that enable me to make best use of my standout strengths are:

Skills and knowledge that might be missing in order for me to get the most from my standout strengths are:

CHAPTER 1.4 – MOVING ON

How to use your strengths more at work

Whatever your role or situation, there will always be ways that you can use your strengths even more effectively than you are currently doing. Having almost completed the Awareness section of this workbook, you are nearly ready to do so. First, though, a final activity to help you understand how to overcome perceived barriers so that you move onto the next stage of your strengths journey confident that it will be a smooth ride.

Before you start though, it's worth taking a moment to reflect upon the two most common hurdles people face when planning to expand the use of their strengths at work:

■ Mental blocks about how to use their strengths more often or in different ways.

■ Perceiving that their current role (or team, or organisation) does not allow them to use some, or all, of their strengths (because of the nature of what they do, the culture of the organisation, their relationship with their line manager, etc.)

Fear not! Our experience shows that both challenges can be overcome.

This final activity will help.

> **TOP TIP**
>
> Your Strengthscope™ Feedback Report Section 5 contains a number of questions and ideas on how you could use your strengths more fully in your current role. For each strength, a number of these ideas are presented. Use these to consider ways in which you could use your strengths more effectively.

Activity 7 – My Work Wheel

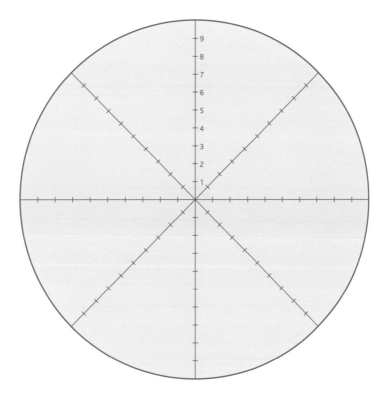

The graphic above illustrates your work wheel. This activity will help you to understand what you need to do to ensure that the rest of your strengths journey is a smooth ride.

1   Identify the eight areas of your current job that you think are most important and label each segment of your work wheel accordingly. Typical labels include team work, customer relationship/account management, business development/sales, administration, project management, report-writing, leading a team, negotiating, research and development, etc.

2   With the centre of the wheel as 0 and the outer edge as an ideal 10, rank your level of positive energy with each job element. Remember that 10 is high and 0 is low.

3   Draw a straight or curved line connecting the *spokes* of the segment.

The new perimeter of the circle represents your work wheel. How bumpy would the ride be if this were a real wheel?

4   Next, please complete the following sentences:

The percentage of my overall time currently allocated to each of the eight main areas of my job is:

In order to strengthen my results at work, this allocation needs to look like this in the future:

I currently enjoy and find these areas of my job energising, because:

I currently find these areas of my job draining, because:

I currently find these areas of my job to be the most stretching, because:

Areas not shown on my wheel that I would like to see in future are:

TOP TIP

Some people find discussing their strengths with others provides them with insight that they wouldn't have experienced had they tried to think through the options on their own. You may find that the insights provided by your colleagues in your Strengthscope™ Feedback Report reflect this. If so, why not talk to other people to get their ideas on creative ways you could apply your strengths.

SUMMARY: SECTION 1 – AWARENESS

1   A strength is a personal characteristic or quality that makes you feel energised and enthusiastic and leads to you doing great work. Becoming fully aware of your strengths is the first step towards putting them to good use.

2   Your Strengthscope™ Feedback Report tells you about your Significant 7 Strengths. You have now focussed in on your Top 3 Strengths which give you the most energy.

3   The more you think, talk and read about these strengths, the closer you will get to understanding what energises you. Considering why certain activities energise you and why others drain you is important. Your Strengthscope™ Feedback Report can help.

4   Having completed all activities, you should now have greater clarity on what it is that you are naturally drawn to and energised by at work. You may also have some ideas about why.

5   In order for your strengths to be productive, they need to be combined with relevant knowledge and skills and translated into productive habits that bring value to the organisation.

6   By thinking about each element of your job, and your positive energy with it, you can start to consider how to use one or more of your strengths more effectively.

My Strengths Plan

The most important things I need to work on based on my learning so far are:

Further reading and references
- Buckingham, M. and Clifton, D.O. (2001). *Now, Discover Your Strengths.* New York: Free Press.
- Gladwell, M. (2005). *Blink: The Power of Thinking Without Thinking.* London, UK: Allen Lane.
- Higgs, M.J. and Dulewicz, S.V. (1998). *Emotional Intelligence: Managerial Fad or Valid Construct?* Henley UK, Henley Working Paper Series, HWP 9813.
- Pegg, M. (2007). *The Strengths Way.* Management Books 2000.

SECTION 2
ACTION

Peak performers go further than purely becoming aware of their strengths. They focus effort over many months and years to sharpen their strengths, translating awareness into action. This section helps you to do just that.

CHAPTER 2.1 – DEVELOPING YOUR STRENGTHS

So far, you have been focusing on gaining an understanding of strengths and using them more in your current role. Peak performers go further. They deliberately develop and SHARPEN their strengths and skills through focused effort over many months and years.

This section sets out the Strengthscope™ SHARPEN model, comprising seven activities to help you get the most out of your strengths and translate awareness into action.

> "Excellence is an art won by training and habituation."
>
> Aristotle, C4th

S	**S**ET SPECIFIC GOALS	What specific goals will help you get more from your strengths and improve your contribution to your team and the organisation?
H	**H**ARNESS ENERGY	How can you harness your energy to give yourself the best possible chance to achieve these specific goals?
A	**A**CQUIRE FLOW	What new skills, knowledge and experience do you need to acquire in order to enter *flow*, enjoying the full benefit of your strengths?
R	**R**EDUCE LIMITING WEAKNESSES	What limiting weaknesses, which get in the way of peak performance, need to be removed or mitigated?
P	**P**RACTICE STRENGTHS AND PRODUCTIVE HABITS	What opportunities will enable you to practice using your strengths and productive habits?
E	**E**NROL SUPPORT	Who can you enrol to support your development and help you optimise your strengths and career success?
N	**N**EXT STEPS	What are the next steps in putting your learning and commitments into action?

Let's go...

CHAPTER 2.2 – SETTING SPECIFIC GOALS

What specific goals will help you get more from your strengths and improve your contribution to your team and the organisation?

To develop your strengths, skills and experience in a way that is valuable for you and your organisation, it is vital to set specific goals.

In crafting such goals it is important to be mindful that, for your strengths to be productive, they should be aligned with your organisation's vision and goals. Doing so ensures that your strengths are being used in a way that creates real value for customers and stakeholders. This, in turn, will increase your chances of success.

The next activity helps you to set such goals.

Here's an example of the level of detail you need to aspire to.

The career or development goal that is most important to me to achieve by   12 / 12 / 11   is:

> To sharpen my courage strength by contributing to 3 hot topic debates each of which leads to at least one change in the way we do things around here.

When I have achieved this, these are the specific things that I will feel, see happening, or hear people saying:

> I will feel proud, strong and more confident to contribute in this way again.
> I will see people doing things differently, perhaps even playing to their own strengths!
> People will say "I can't believe we didn't do this before. It makes my life so much easier!";
> "It took courage to suggest these changes. Do you have any other ideas?"

TOP TIP

Being as specific as possible in setting your goals and describing how you will feel, what will be happening and what people will be saying when these goals have been reached is the key to getting the most out of this activity. Using this kind of visualisation technique enables top sportspeople to prepare mentally for a successful performance, giving themselves higher levels of motivation and the best possible chance of success.

Activity 8 – Setting My Strengths Goals

Please complete the following sentences:

The career or development goal that is most important to me to achieve by   /   /   is:

When I have achieved this, these are the specific things that I will feel, see happening, or hear people saying:

Things I value deeply, which I will not give up or compromise in pursuing this goal, are:

The way this will create specific value for my organisation and its customers is:

When I achieve this goal, the specific advantages for me and my career will be:

CHAPTER 2.3 – HARNESSING YOUR ENERGY

How can you harness your energy to give yourself the best possible chance to achieve the specific goals you have set for yourself?

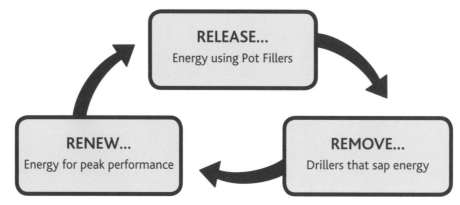

Activity 9 – Harnessing Your Energy

Release Energy Using Pot Fillers

In Activity 3, you considered *pot fillers* and *pot drillers* in relation to your life and work.

In building productive habits and performing at your best, it is important to think once again of yourself as this *pot* of energy.

A *pot filler* is anything that brings you encouragement and positive energy, whether this is a person, an object or an activity.

In the spaces below, write your 5 most important pot fillers in your life above the dotted line, e.g. people, things or activities.

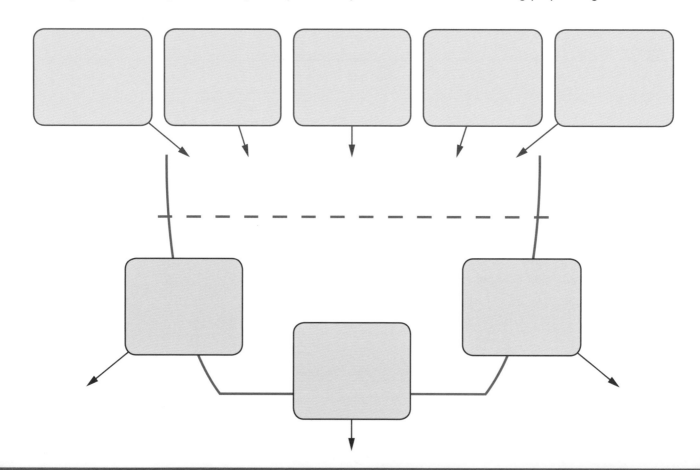

There are numerous ways to increase the energy in your pot. Here are some ideas:

- Clarify your purpose and values (some of the activities later in the workbook may help with this)
- Spend more time playing to your strengths
- Develop your skills and knowledge in areas of strength
- Spend more time with people who make you feel more confident and energised
- Spend more time on activities that recharge or re-energise you outside of work

With reference to your pot, please complete the following sentences:

The specific things I can do to fill my pot are:

1.

2.

3.

The way my strengths can help include:

1.

2.

3.

Remove Drillers That Sap Energy

A *pot driller* is anything that brings unhappiness and stress, that drains you or saps your energy, whether this is a person, a thing or an activity.

On your pot diagram on the previous page, write down your 3 most significant pot drillers.

Examples of ways to reduce pot drillers include:

- Letting go of work that can be done better by others
- Working on limiting weaknesses or overdone strengths (more on this in Chapter 3)
- Improving relations and communication with your manager and colleagues
- Building in more time for important activities, rather than spending too much of your time on draining ones
- Removing persistent barriers and blockers to effective job performance

The specific things I can do to deal with the holes in my pot are:

> 1.
>
> 2.
>
> 3.

The way my strengths can help include:

> 1.
>
> 2.
>
> 3.

Renew Energy for Peak Performance

To sustain performance and remain *in the zone*, we need to balance our *energy spend* with an intermittent recharging of our batteries.

If we don't recharge, we may just end up *surviving* or even worse, *burning out*. Finding opportunities to relax and do things we find really energising outside of work is important to our long term health and success.
The way that each person goes about this renewal and achieves a healthy, fulfilled life is very different depending on their needs, values and personality.

There are 3 main areas of our life we need to consider when looking at renewal and sustained peak performance:

Me Time

This is the time you spend by yourself outside of work doing what you love to do. This could be participating in a hobby, sport or pastime, but it could equally be time relaxing, meditating or just enjoying being alive.

Work Time

This is all the time you spend working, regardless of whether this is at the office, at home or travelling for work and after hours on the laptop and other electronic devices!

Family/Friend Time

This is the time you spend with and on your family, as a wife, husband, partner, parent, son, daughter, brother, sister, friend, etc.

TOP TIP

It's important to note that the aim here is not necessarily to achieve balance in the different areas of your life, but to achieve an overall gain in positive energy which will lead to sustainable success.

Many people lead long, happy and energised lives with little balance. What they do achieve, however, is a purposeful and positive life involving making the most of their strengths, skills and knowledge.

In the left hand box below, draw a circle and divide it into the 3 *life areas* shown in the picture on the previous page. The size of each of the segments should reflect the amount of time you currently devote to each of these areas of your life.

In the right hand box, redraw the circle. Now divide it into the 3 life areas, with each segment size now reflecting the ideal allocation of time that will enable you to maximise your positive energy and success at work, but also in life more generally.

Consider what you have drawn before you and answer the following questions:

The specific things I choose to do to move towards my ideal allocation of time are:

1.

by   /   /

2.

by   /   /

3.

by   /   /

The benefits of making this move are:

Me...

My organisation...

My family/friends...

The consequences and risks of staying where I am are:

CHAPTER 2.4 – ACHIEVING FLOW

What new skills, knowledge and experience do you need to acquire in order to enter *flow*, enjoying the full benefit of your strengths?

In Section 1 we suggested that strengths offer the promise of peak performance. Strengths alone, though, will not deliver peak performance. Peak performance requires entering a state known as *flow*. To enter *flow* you need to identify and acquire skills, knowledge and experience relevant to each of your strengths.

Section 5 of your Strengthscope™ Feedback Report, *Making the Most of Your Strengths*, offers various questions to help you do this. It is by no means a complete list, but discussing such options with your manager is a great start. Understanding the concept of *flow* is also important. The following activity helps. First though, a little more about *flow*.

What is *flow*?

Flow is an optimal state of motivation and performance, where the person is fully immersed in what he or she is doing.

World-renowned professor Mihaly Csíkszentmihályi (1990), a leader in the field of positive psychology and the first to develop the concept of *flow*, described the feeling as *"being completely involved in an activity for its own sake. The ego falls away. Time flies. Every action, movement, and thought follows inevitably from the previous one. Your whole being is involved, and you're using your skills to the utmost."*

Peak performance occurs when there is a good match between a person's strengths and skills and the challenge of the task/activity they undertake. If the task is too easy, or too difficult, *flow* cannot occur. Similarly, if a person doesn't have the strengths or skills for the task/activity, peak performance and learning is unlikely to occur.

Let's see how your strengths and skills match the tasks you have to undertake in your daily work...

Activity 10 – My Work Flow

1   Referring back to Activity 7, *My Work Wheel*, place your key daily activities on the *Flow* Diagram[2] below, based on the level of challenge you associate with each and the level of relevant skill you perceive you have for each.

2   Think about each task/activity and why it is positioned where it is on the diagram. Try and identify the underlying reasons for:

a   Tasks/activities in flow
b   Tasks/activities where your skills are perceived to be greater than the challenge of the task (where you feel complacent or bored)
c   Tasks/activities where challenge is perceived to be greater than the skills (where you feel anxious or stressed).

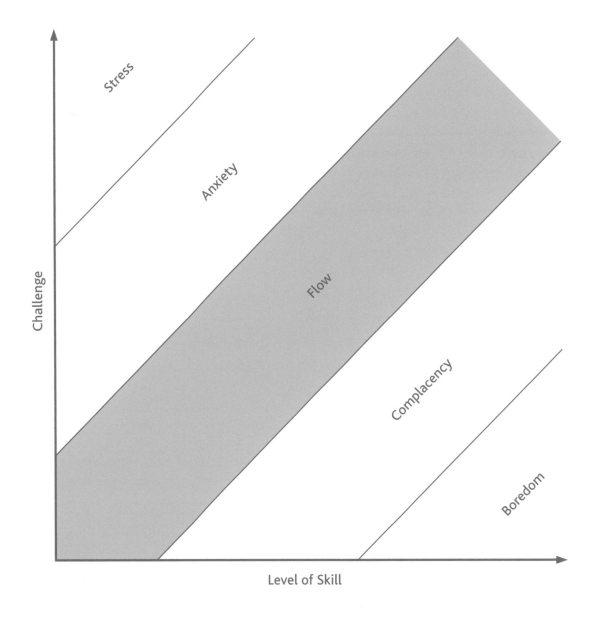

2   Thanks to Simon Shellard for his practical development of the *flow* concept, as reproduced here.

For those activities falling into the *flow* area of the diagram (activities where you feel at ease and excel, where you are in your element), please complete the following table:

> These are the daily activities where I experience *flow*. Specifically, this is what I am doing when I experience *flow* in my work day:
>
>
>
> These are the specific results my team and organisation see from my *flow* activities:
>
>
>
> These are the skills and strengths I apply when I am in *flow*:

For activities falling into the areas on the *Flow* Diagram where the challenge was greater than the skill (where you felt anxious or stressed), there are several strategies you could consider using to bring these tasks closer to the *flow* zone, including:

- Enhancing, improving or developing your skills in these areas
- Breaking down these specific tasks into more manageable chunks
- Getting help from others who have more appropriate strengths, or greater skill levels.

Considering the above ideas, complete the following sentence. In order to bring work activities which are leading me to feel anxious or stressed closer to *flow*, I will...

> 1.
>
> 2.
>
> 3.

For activities falling into the areas of the *Flow* Diagram where your skill is greater than the challenge (where you feel complacent or bored), there are some other approaches which could help bring these closer to *flow*, including:

- Increasing the challenge of these activities by increasing their difficulty
- Training or mentoring others in developing skill in this area of activity
- Considering applying your skills in these areas to different, more challenging tasks

Considering the above ideas, complete the following sentence. In order to bring work activities which are leading me to feel complacent or bored closer to *flow*, I will...

1.

2.

3.

It is well worth sharing your thoughts on *flow* with your manager and/or work colleagues. Specifically, you could let your manager know which tasks are currently in *flow* and which fall outside the *flow* zone, so that you can work together on bringing more of your work activities close to *flow*. Although it's hard to get 100% of your work tasks in *flow*, you can increase your percentage from its current point... your manager and colleagues may be able to help with this.

CHAPTER 2.5 – REDUCING LIMITING WEAKNESSES

You're really gaining momentum now! So far in this Action section of the workbook, you have discovered how to:

- Set your specific personal development goals
- Harness enough energy to enable you to achieve these goals
- Acquire the skills, knowledge and experience necessary to help you *flow*

Spotting Limiting Weaknesses

Up until now, we've focused almost solely on strengths and successes. This is how high performers achieve success. But they don't ignore weaknesses, particularly ones we call limiting weaknesses.

Everyone has both strengths and weaknesses in just the same way that for every mountain peak, there is a valley. However, not all weaknesses are the same in terms of their impact on performance and success.

But what are limiting weaknesses and how do they differ from their less troublesome partners, allowable weaknesses?

Spotting limiting weaknesses is relatively easy. They can:

- Be areas in which we are unlikely to be able to sustain high performance
- Be a persistent source of problems and mistakes
- Have the potential to undermine our performance and career
- Be perceived by our colleagues as weaker areas or limitations
- Drain our energy or leave us feeling cold
- Be *strengths in overdrive* which are perceived by colleagues as weaknesses (more on this in Chapter 3)

On the other hand, allowable weaknesses typically have a minor or negligible impact on performance and success. People are generally prepared to overlook these as they are regarded as minor flaws or annoying habits.

Now look through your Strengthscope™ profile for the lower bars in your strengths profile in Section 3. Some of these may represent limiting weaknesses. Some may represent allowable weaknesses. Some may not represent weaknesses at all, but should be regarded as *non strengths*, or areas which do not energise us but just leave us feeling neutral or drained.

It is important to draw a distinction between these types of weakness, rather than putting them all in the same pot – while we can probably live with allowable weaknesses, we might well be wise to do something about limiting ones. But we should be realistic about how important these weaknesses really are in holding us back from achieving success.

For many of us, limiting weaknesses show up in deeply ingrained toxic behaviours or habits. These become difficult to change, but the good news is that they can be improved or reduced with determination and lots of practice.

It is important to understand and accept our weaker areas, as well as putting together actions for reducing any negative outcomes associated with the limiting ones.

The aim here is for balance. We need to amplify and build on our distinctive strengths while at the same time reducing limiting weaknesses and strengths in overdrive, which we will cover in Section 3.

Balancing Act

Reducing Limiting Weaknesses

So how do we reduce limiting weaknesses?

There are various ways including:

- Acquiring new skills, knowledge and behaviour to build out the weaker area
- Putting disciplines in place to avoid toxic or unproductive habits and reminding yourself of these everyday
- Bringing in people who can complement you in areas where you have a weakness
- Securing a coach or mentor to help you improve
- Finding opportunities on and off the job to practice new work habits that lessen the impact of the weakness
- Using one or more of your strengths to compensate, as this can give you energy to draw from while working on the weakness.

Discuss these options with your manager, coach and/or mentor to find the best actions that fit your situation, strengths and personal style.

Working on reducing limiting weaknesses is far from easy. In fact, it is perfectly natural to experience frustrations, setbacks and negative energy during the change process, especially in the first few months.

However, with clear actions, a strong desire to change and finding creative ways to use your strengths to overcome or mitigate limiting weaknesses, you should be able to improve to at least a level where these weaknesses won't undermine job performance and career success.

Activity 11 – Reducing Limiting Weaknesses

Complete the worksheet to identify some of your limiting weaknesses together with actions you can take to reduce their impact:

Limiting weakness	Impact on...		Strengths that I can use to compensate or make the weakness less relevant	Specific actions I will take
	Me	My team/My organisation		
1.				
2.				
3.				

CHAPTER 2.6 – DEVELOPING STRENGTHS AND PRODUCTIVE HABITS

OK. So you understand the anatomy of your strengths, you have set some specific goals and you have begun to take action to ensure that you have sufficient energy reserves to achieve these goals. Now it's time to start consciously and deliberately practising specific behaviours and habits which will allow you to get the most from your strengths.

Now's the opportunity to be more deliberate in developing behaviours and productive habits that will take your strengths and ultimately your work performance and career potential to the next level.

The following activities encourage you to explore three proven methods for creating new opportunities to stretch yourself and develop your strengths:

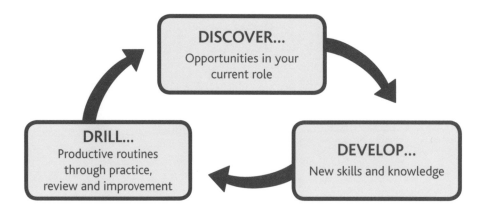

Activity 12 - Discover Opportunities in Your Current Role... and Beyond

A rich seam of untapped opportunities for greater use of your strengths often lies within your current job. What needs to be done is to find time to explore (with your manager and other co-workers) the extent to which you can perform your role in a way that enables you to perform tasks and take on responsibilities that are in line with your strengths. Before booking your meeting to discuss this with your boss or team though, take ten minutes to consider the following.

How can you perform the key elements of your role differently, enabling you to use your strengths to a greater extent?

For example, as for many of us, there were administrative tasks required of James's role. While he gained little energy from *detail orientation* or *efficiency* (these were non strengths for James), his *creativity* and *initiative* strengths enabled him to look at these administrative tasks in a new and different way, quickly building momentum around getting them done using his new approach.

Bearing this example in mind, please complete the following table:

My role involves these key elements...	I can use my strengths differently to get these tasks done by...

You may also want to consider how you can use some of your strengths outside of work. Taking on activities outside work that help you build on your strengths can provide valuable learning opportunities. For example, someone with a *leading* strength but with little opportunity to take on a leadership position at work might volunteer as a leader of a scout group, sports club, parents' association or local charity.

Please complete the following table for each of your Top 3 strengths:

My Top 3 strengths are:	Ways I can apply these strengths outside of work include:

Activity 13 – Develop Skills and Knowledge in Areas of Strength

If you look back at Activity 6, *Optimised vs Sub-optimised strengths*, you will have noted down some skills and knowledge that allow you to get the best from your strengths, but also some skills and knowledge that might be missing.

This is the chance for you to put together a plan outlining how you will develop the skills and knowledge that give you the best possible return when using your strengths. Focus on those strengths that you feel will benefit the most from you gaining new skills.

TOP TIP

Research tells us that we need 10,000 hours to truly master a new skill – this equates to over 5 years of full time working hours dedication! The good news with strengths is that you already have a running start. Because you are naturally drawn towards using your strengths, it is highly likely that you will have already learned some productive habits around them.

For example, Petra found that she was very energised when she got the chance to use her *strategic mindedness* strength at work. But her suggestions in meetings weren't necessarily hitting the mark. By gaining new knowledge and skills in business analysis and applying strategy models to support her suggestions, Petra was able to make a much greater impact with her strength... and she had never felt more energised at work!

For each of your 3 standout strengths, identify skills and knowledge you can develop or acquire to build out and optimise your strengths at work. Like Petra, try to think of *stretch* opportunities that will raise your contribution as well as your energy levels.

Strength 1:

Skill or knowledge area I can improve/acquire:

How does this help me get the most from my strength?

Where can I look for ways of gaining the skills and knowledge?

Where will I apply this new skill or knowledge once I have acquired it?

Strength 2:

Skill or knowledge area I can improve/acquire:

How does this help me get the most from my strength?

Where can I look for ways of gaining the skills and knowledge?

Where will I apply this new skill or knowledge once I have acquired it?

Strength 3:

Skill or knowledge area I can improve/acquire:

How does this help me get the most from my strength?

Where can I look for ways of gaining the skills and knowledge?

Where will I apply this new skill or knowledge once I have acquired it?

Activity 14 – Drill Your Strengths with Regular Practice, Review and Improvement

The latest neuroscience research tells us that the more we practice a new skill or behaviour, the quicker electrical impulses are transmitted along that neural pathway and the better we get at that activity. So practice really does make perfect![*]

One of the challenges here is that you might be taking your strengths for granted without subjecting them to the same level of practice that you would give to, say, learning a new sport or using a new computer application.

There will be some new ways of working, new ways of thinking and new applications of knowledge that you have identified in the last two activities which will lead to productive, positive behaviour routines. But to get the most from these, you will need to keep reviewing and repeating these positive routines in order to embed them and for them to become habit.

So when the time is right, use the boxes below to review and improve the productive habits you have gained from the earlier activities.

Let's start with an example from Petra:

Productive Habit 1:	*Using SWOT and PESTLE analysis to strengthen suggestions*

Where have I used this?
In our team meeting when discussing our strategy for stakeholder engagement

What was the outcome?
Our final strategy included opportunities that we wouldn't have considered before and also reflected upcoming funding changes in the organisation, which we hadn't fully considered.

Is there anything I would do differently next time?
I could have circulated my report before the meeting, which would have given us more time to consider options rather than reading through my report.

Where is the next opportunity to try this out?
At our next review meeting in 2 months. I would also like to try out 'scenario planning' around the different stakeholder groups to see what we come up with.

TOP TIP

Daniel Coyle, in his book The Talent Code, talks about how this process of learning new skills actually works in the brain. Coyle says:

"*(1) Every human movement, thought, or feeling is a precisely timed electric signal traveling through a chain of neurons – a circuit of nerve fibers. (2) Myelin is the insulation that wraps these nerve fibers and increases signal strength, speed, and accuracy. (3) The more we fire a particular circuit, the more myelin optimizes that circuit, and the stronger, faster, and more fluent our movements and thoughts become.*"

The importance of this finding is that we need to keep repeating and practising new skills and different ways of thinking if they are to *stick* and become our normal way of doing things – this is particularly true of practising new productive habits based on strengths.

Here is some space to record your own experiences:

Productive Habit 1:

Where have I used this?

What was the outcome?

Is there anything I would do differently next time?

Where is the next opportunity to try this out?

Productive Habit 2:

Where have I used this?

What was the outcome?

Is there anything I would do differently next time?

Where is the next opportunity to try this out?

Don't forget to practice, review and improve your productive habits based on strengths, building these out into your everyday work tasks. The more you do this, the better you will get at playing to your strengths. You will also find that you get more back in return – for yourself, your work colleagues and for your organisation overall.

And remember, practice really does make perfect!

CHAPTER 2.7 – ENROLLING SUPPORT

Who can you enrol to support your development and help you optimise your strengths and career success?

Enrolling support to help you apply your strengths and practice new productive habits will improve your self-confidence and provide feedback and reassurance that you are on the right track.

Often, people think too narrowly about sources of support when they are seeking people to help with their development. Those closest to you, at home and in work, are typically those that spring to mind first, but are not always the best people to provide input to help you develop your strengths.

When considering those who might be able to support you, think about the role they can best play.

Helpful support roles include:

Coach:	This person typically provides focused support to help you acquire a specific skill, consider new opportunities for learning and development, and overcome particular challenges to full performance.
Feedback-giver:	This person is in a good position to observe your behaviour and give you honest and constructive feedback about what they have observed.
Mentor:	This person provides longer-term support and guidance through sharing their wisdom, experience and learning.
Sponsor:	This person opens up opportunities for you to move into new areas at work and promotes your profile and work within the organisation.
Supporter:	This person expresses strong confidence in your abilities and potential, and energises you to grow and succeed.

Of course, some people you choose to support you can take on more than one role (e.g. Mentor AND Sponsor, Coach AND Supporter).

Let's map your own personal strengths support network...

Activity 15 – My Strengths Support Network

Example of a Stakeholder Support Map

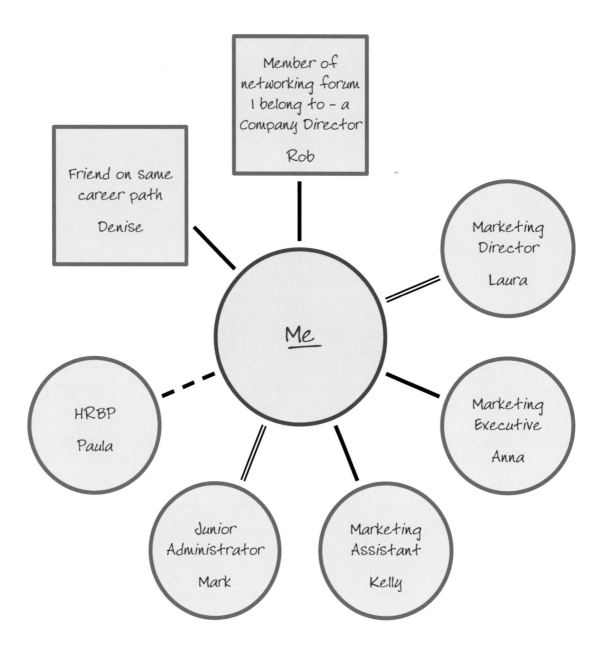

1   Please draw a circle to represent yourself in the space below.

2   Think about your co-workers. Who do you think may be able to help you in developing your strengths? Arrange them around you in circles. Place the people you think will be most supportive closest to you and the people who will provide less support further away.

3   Try to keep the formal organisation structure by placing people higher in the organisation above you on the map, people lower in the organisation below you on the map and colleagues to either side of you.

4   Place other stakeholders who may be able to provide support for your development in boxes rather than circles.

5   Connect each person to you using the following code (see diagram on page 44 as an example):
    • DOUBLE LINES mean you are currently getting a lot of value from the relationship
    • SINGLE LINES mean you are currently getting some value from the relationship
    • DOTTED LINES mean you are currently getting very little or no value from the relationship

6   With reference to your map, please complete the following sentences:

These people are best placed to help me build the skills, knowledge and experience to optimise my strengths

This is the specific support each of these key people can provide:

7   Map this information on to the table below, adding your desired outcome in the final column.

Support person	Role	Desired outcome
1.		
2.		
3.		
4.		
5.		

8   Please complete the following sentences:

These people are best placed to provide me with complementary strengths and perspectives,
enabling me to improve on and compensate for my weaker areas:

I need to build stronger relations with these people in order to get more of their time and attention:

CHAPTER 2.8 – NEXT STEPS

What are the next steps in putting your learning and commitments into action?

Congratulations, you are nearly ready to move beyond action, towards the next part of your strength journey, building agility into your routine. First though, it's time to commit!

Translating your learning from your Strengthscope™ Feedback Report and the activities in this workbook requires firm commitments about what you intend to change, as well as specific actions to guide follow-through. Commitments can be easily broken though, especially if they are not realistic or are not shared with others who can remind you of your pledge.

The next and final step in this section, involves reviewing your learning to date and sharing your commitments with the people who are supporting your development (as well as other people important to you, including close friends and family members).

Let's write your Strengths Development Action Plan…

Activity 16 – My Strengths Development Action Plan

Using the table on the next page, please record your strengths development action plan, ensuring that any goals you set are SMART, or SMARTER. Remember to note down:

- How each commitment will help you and the organisation
- Your specific action plan
- Review dates for each commitment
- Any support you may need

S	M	A	R	T	E	R					
SPECIFIC	MEASURABLE	ACHIEVABLE	RELEVANT	TIMEBOUND	EVALUATED	REVIEWED
I will...						
I will...						
I will...						
I will...						

SUMMARY: SECTION 2 – ACTION

1   Successful people work hard to SHARPEN their strengths and skills through focused effort and deliberate practice over a long period of time.

2   Peak performance and *flow* experiences happen when there is a good match between a person's strengths and skills and the challenges of the task/activity they are undertaking.

3   Spotting and reducing your limiting weaknesses will reduce the risks of poor performance and failure. Although this is rarely easy, it is possible to improve in areas of weakness. If you remain focused and have a strong will to succeed, you will find creative ways to use your strengths to overcome limiting weaknesses.

4   Building broad support to help you apply your strengths and practice new productive habits is essential to improve your self-confidence and your energy level. It also provides you with feedback and reassurance that you are on the right track.

5   Translating your learning from your Strengthscope™ Feedback Report and the exercises in this workbook requires firm commitments about what you intend to change, as well as specific actions to guide follow-through.

My Strengths Plan

My key learning points from this section, the most important things I need to work on are:

Further reading and references
- Coyle, D. (2009). *The Talent Code: Greatness Isn't Born. It's Grown. Here's How.* New York: Bantam Dell.
- Csíkszentmihályi, M. (1990). *Flow: The Psychology of Optimal Experience.* Harper Collins.
- Gladwell, M. (2008). *Outliers.* Little, Brown and Company.

SECTION 3
AGILITY

It may surprise you to learn that you can overplay your strengths; strengths can go into overdrive with less than positive outcomes. Using your strengths in an agile, balanced way to get the best possible result, and communicating these results in acceptable and memorable ways, is the key to sustaining peak performance. This section helps you to do just that.

CHAPTER 3.1 – USING STRENGTHS IN BALANCE

Preventing strengths going into *overdrive*

Making the most of your strengths at work, means taking productive actions that result in you achieving your personal and work goals. Sometimes, however, strengths can go into overdrive, resulting in unintended and unexpected consequences.

For example, someone with a *courage* strength who doesn't sufficiently understand the political subtleties and sensitivities of a situation may come across as arrogant, or overly forceful in the way they challenge established ways of doing things.

Similarly, someone who is strongly energised by *critical thinking* may come across to their colleagues as overly negative or pessimistic when a more upbeat, creative problem-solving approach is preferable.

Research shows that it is often not the absence of a skill or competency that leads to failure or *derailment* at work. Rather, it is our strengths in overdrive. We find what works for us, and because these strengths and familiar behavioural routines generally result in positive outcomes, we use them again and again.

Using them in this way though, can result in unintended and undesirable consequences. By failing to spot when our strengths are going into overdrive, and the triggers of these negative habits and behaviours, we are likely to end up falling short of our goals and attracting negative feedback.

This in turn can undermine our confidence and self-image, which puts us into a performance tailspin, leading to further problems and at worst, the loss of our job.

Think of the effective use of strengths as adjusting the volume dial on a sound system. When the volume is turned up too loud, it can distort the music and be harmful to our ears, i.e. it can go into overdrive. The volume also needs to take account of the situation you are in. For example, if you are in a train carriage, the volume will probably be much lower than when you are enjoying music at the gym or a party.

Like adjusting the volume when you are listening to a favourite piece of music, it is important to adjust the volume on your strength to get the most out of each situation. Learning how to *dial-up* and *dial-down* your strengths plays an important part in ensuring they are used productively and help you be your best.

> **"Nothing in excess"**
>
> Oracle at Delphi, C5th BCE

Situational factors that could result in your strengths going into overdrive if not taken into account include:

- Personality and expectations of stakeholders
- Culture and values of the work group/organisation
- Size, structure and strategy of the work group/organisation
- Leadership beliefs and style
- Nature of the task/project
- Workload
- Policies, procedures and systems
- Market and customers' needs

Below are five clues you should watch out for which may indicate that your strengths are in overdrive:

1   You receive mixed feedback on your strengths, skills and performance from your co-workers/stakeholders

2   You appear to be performing well, but are getting average or mixed performance reviews or appraisals from your manager

3   You are being passed over for assignments or promotion opportunities, particularly those which are important, and more visible to key decision-makers

4   You struggle to maintain a consistent level of performance in new or unfamiliar situations

5   You struggle to move outside your *comfort zone* and approach new assignments and situations with skill and confidence.

A final tip is to rely on the old-fashioned principle of consideration or courtesy in the way you apply your strengths at work and home. When you use your greatest strengths, you should ensure you protect others from any inappropriate or overuse of the strength.

In other words, don't turn your music up too loudly when you're sitting in a packed train carriage, as this is likely to be irritating to others and may lead to unintended or unwanted consequences.

Let's take a look at what your strengths in overdrive might look like...

Activity 17 – My Strengths in Overdrive

Based on your Strengthscope™ profile, identify three strengths from your *Significant 7* that you feel go into overdrive, either regularly or occasionally and write them in the boxes below.

Strength 1:	Strength 2:	Strength 3:

For each, map out what your behaviour looks like in the *Peak Performance Zone* (i.e. when you are performing well, achieving your goals) and in *Overdrive* by completing the sentences below.

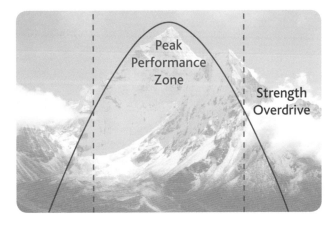

The consequences when each strength goes into overdrive for me, my team, my organisation and for people outside of work are:

Strength 1:

Me:

My team:

My organisation:

Others:

Strength 2:

Me:

My team:

My organisation:

Others:

Strength 3:

Me:

My team:

My organisation:

Others:

The specific situational factors that cause each strength to go into overdrive are:

Strength 1:

Strength 2:

Strength 3:

The benefits of staying in the peak performance zone more often for you, me, my team, my organisation and people outside of work include:

Strength 1:

Me:
My team:
My organisation:
Others:

Strength 2:

Me:
My team:
My organisation:
Others:

Strength 3:

Me:
My team:
My organisation:
Others:

Things I need to do more of, less of, or do differently to prevent each strength from going into overdrive include:

Strength 1:

Strength 2:

Strength 3:

I will know when I've been successful in using each strength in a more flexible, balanced way because these specific things will be happening:

Strength 1:

Strength 2:

Strength 3:

TOP TIP

Managing your strengths from going into overdrive requires building positive and weeding out toxic routines. Referring back to *Activity 9. Harnessing Your Energy*, *Activity 11. Reducing Limiting Weaknesses* and the activities in *Chapter 2.5. Developing Strengths and Productive Habits* will help.

CHAPTER 3.2 – COMMUNICATING YOUR STRENGTHS

So far you have become fully aware of your strengths, what energises you and what drains you of energy; you have taken a series of steps to put your strengths into action and you have considered how to prevent yourself from overusing your strengths, from pushing your strengths into overdrive.

How, though, do you communicate your strengths in a way that people can accept and that will enable you to flourish?

Let's talk personal brand...

Branding is all around us. The way products are branded is fundamental to how we perceive them. It influences our choices. Branding also applies to people. We all have a personal brand (what other people think of us and the value they believe we bring to work and relationships). Some people don't like the idea of a *personal brand* though, as it smacks of self-promotion and self-interest. Whether we like it or not, we all have one, so we may as well embrace it. Why?

Because building our *brand* (or promise) and communicating it to others, helps us:

1   To differentiate ourselves in a highly competitive internal and external marketplace;
2   To increase our visibility in the company and make others aware of our presence;
3   To ensure people have a clear sense of who we are and how to work with us;
4   To become more self-confident and self motivated as we gain in self-awareness and what we have to offer.

Strong personal brands are not built overnight. They take a long time to evolve and require consistency and continuous reinforcement. It's worth it though, as all great brands produce strong results in terms of improved demand, perceived product/service value, reputation and results.

So, what do you want people to say about you when you are not in the room?

> "Your brand is what people say about you when you are not in the room"
>
> Jeff Bezos, founder of Amazon, C21st

Activity 18 – Communicating My Strengths

From all your work to date, take a moment to reflect on the strengths that you see as most fundamental to you and your success at work. Focusing in on your Top 3, consider not only how and why they energise you, but also what contribution they can make to your organisation. Completing the sentences below, describe this contribution in a way that will be understood and appreciated by other people, particularly those people who are in the most influential roles with regards to your job and career success.

Strength 1:
This strength contributes value to my organisation in these ways:
I can describe this strength to my most important stakeholders at work so they understand this value in these ways:

Strength 2
This strength contributes value to my organisation in these ways:
I can describe this strength to my most important stakeholders at work so they understand this value in these ways:

Strength 3
This strength contributes value to my organisation in these ways:
I can describe this strength to my most important stakeholders at work so they understand this value in these ways:

TOP TIP

The way that you describe and communicate your strengths so that others can understand the contribution you can make is similar to the current thinking on writing a Curriculum Vitae: that it is best to describe outcomes you have achieved in a role and weave in how you achieved those outcomes. So for example 'My *collaboration* strength has enabled me to build a network of productive supplier relationships from scratch, enabling my company to save £500k in overhead costs'

Activity 19 – My Brand Pyramid

A brand pyramid is a tool used by branding professionals to clarify and control their messages. It can also be a powerful tool enabling you to communicate and control your personal brand.

Take Kalvin, a senior sales manager whose Top 3 Strengthscope™ strengths were *strategic mindedness*, *results focus* and *relationship building*. Following the steps below, Kalvin crafted his brand pyramid, distilling his brand essence down to "bringing value to your business".

Everyone agreed, "Yes, that is exactly what Kalvin does," even his line manager, who offered to retain him at a level which enabled him to make the leap across to self employment (his personal goal in his strengths plan). Not wishing to miss out on the action, two existing contacts in his professional network contracted him to deliver specific partnership projects too.

Kalvin's Brand Pyramid

By simply clarifying and communicating his goals and brand to three key stakeholders, Kalvin was successful in carving himself a niche career which played, totally, to his strengths.

Let's now look at your brand...

Step 1: Review the values you wrote down as being important to you in *Activity 8, Setting My Strengths Goals* (under the section *"Things I value deeply, which I will not give up or compromise in pursuing this goal, are:"*).

Please complete the following sentence:

These are my personal values. I feel so passionately about them that I will not give them up or compromise them in pursuing my goals:

Value 1:

Value 2:

Value 3:

Value 4:

Step 2: Identify the strengths you believe reflect your values and passions most authentically (there will be clues in the feedback you have received from colleagues in your Strengthscope™ Feedback Report; there will also be clues in reviewing the Strengthscope™ descriptions of your *Significant 7 Strengths*):

My standout strengths when I am in *flow*, at one and enjoying success are:

TOP TIP

Some people find it helpful to focus in on their values by identifying what it is that makes them angry: For Kalvin, injustice is one trigger (making *fairness* one of his values). People pretending to be something they are not, is another trigger (making *authenticity* a value). Laziness just drives Kalvin mad (hence the *action and delivery* values, which happen to reflect his *results focus* strength, another strong indicator that they are true and deeply held values).

Step 3: Identify your brand personality or proposition. Your brand proposition is what you want people to say about you when you are not in the room. Reflecting the value your strengths can bring to your business in less than 20 words (or 15 seconds), it crystallises your offering. Before trying though, it is worth reviewing your answers to *Activity 18 Communicating My Strengths*.

Ready? Let's do it...

This is my brand proposition it clarifies my strengths and the value I can bring. It is the 20 words (or less) that I would like people to say about me when I am not in the room:

Step 4: Distilling your essence. You brand essence is your strap line: what you'd want people to say about you if they thought you might walk back in the room in the next five seconds! It's how you'd like to be introduced at meetings, your equivalent of L'Oreal's "Because you're worth it" or Nike's "Just do it".

My brand essence, the six words (or less) that I would like people to use to introduce me at meetings is:

Step 5: Draw your brand pyramid. In the space below draw your own brand pyramid, bringing it to life with colour and any creative ideas you may have.

To succeed in today's competitive marketplace, you must be keenly aware of external perceptions of your personality, strengths and your contribution. Inviting feedback from key stakeholders on your brand pyramid and your ongoing performance will enable you to close any gaps between how you aspire to be seen and how you are actually seen.

We hope you're enjoying your strengths journey!

SUMMARY: SECTION 3 – AGILITY

1   Strengths in overdrive can undermine your performance and career if they are not managed effectively. In order to maximise your strengths, you need to learn to use them in a balanced, flexible way, matching them carefully to the needs of different people and work situations.

2   Positive routines or work habits that make your strengths productive, and lead to effective outcomes, don't arise without a lot of perseverance and hard work. By practicing these routines using a combination of on and off the job development including coaching, new work assignments, reflection, feedback and training, you can build the required skills, behaviours and experience to get the most from your strengths.

3   Toxic routines that undermine performance need to be corrected to ensure behaviour doesn't unintentionally lead to poor results and career troubles. Putting in place actions to mitigate and reduce the incidence of these improves your chances of success at work.

4   Your personal brand is what other people think of you and the value they believe you bring to work and relationships. Building and implementing a coherent and consistent personal brand has many advantages including:
    a   Differentiating yourself in a highly competitive internal and external marketplace
    b   Ensuring people have a clear sense of who you are and how to engage with you
    c   Strengthening your confidence and motivation as you become clearer about yourself and what you offer

5   Brands take a long time to evolve and require consistency and continuous reinforcement to grow strong.

6   The most powerful brand to project is an authentic one that you believe truly reflects your strengths and who you really are when you are at your best.

7   To succeed in today's competitive marketplace, you must be keenly aware of external perceptions of your personality, strengths and your contribution. Inviting feedback from key stakeholders will enable you to close any gaps between how you aspire to be seen and how you are actually seen.

My Strengths Plan

My key learning points from this section, the most important things I need to work on are:

Further reading and references

- Colvin, G. (2008). *Talent Is Overrated: What Really Separates World-Class Performers from Everybody Else*. New York: Penguin.
- Coyle, D. (2009). *The Talent Code: Greatness Isn't Born. It's Grown. Here's How*. New York: Bantam Dell.
- Gladwell, M. (2008). *Outliers*. Little, Brown and Company.
- Hopson, Dr B. & Ledger, K. (2010) *And What Do You Do?* A&C Black.
- Montoya, P. and Vandehey, T. (2005). *The Brand Called You*. Personal Branding Press.
- Waldroop, J. & Butler, T. (Sep-Oct, 2000). *Managing Away Bad Habits*. Harvard Business Review OnPoint.
- For more on *leadership brand* and the central role of strengths, see: http://www.youtube.com/watch?v=vtjWXzajQXw

SECTION 4
ACHIEVEMENT

Many of us tend to take our achievements for granted. But peak performers don't only focus on learning from mistakes and shortfalls. They also look for what's working well and find meaningful ways to recognise and celebrate their strengths and achievements. This helps them build confidence and a positive mindset for future success. This section helps you to do the same.

CHAPTER 4.1 – BUILD A CYCLE OF SUCCESS

Recognising and building on achievements

Many of us tend to take our achievements for granted. The aspects of our jobs that play to our strengths and which we excel at are generally easier for us. So, we tend to dismiss them as not being worth a mention. If we remain unaware of how valuable these contributions are, it's easy for us to focus too much on mistakes, problems and weaknesses, which can result in us feeling inadequate and drained. This in turn causes us to see ourselves in a negative light which fuels low expectations and a decline in performance. A vicious, energy sapping cycle is created which undermines our confidence and success.

In the previous sections, we have learned that focusing on our strengths and successes can put us on a very different pathway: one called the *Cycle of Success*.

As the diagram below shows, having a clear understanding of and belief in our strengths, enables us to build a positive view of ourselves. This then raises our expectations of what we can achieve and improves our chances of success.

> ## "It's not the mountain we conquer, but ourselves"
>
> Edmund Hillary

Cycle of Success

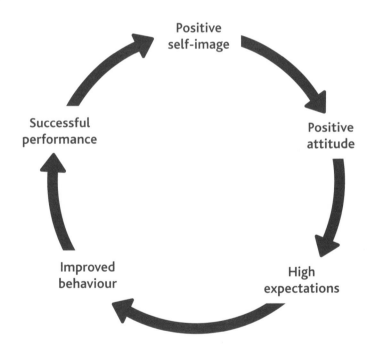

Positive self-image → Positive attitude → High expectations → Improved behaviour → Successful performance → (back to Positive self-image)

This all sounds good in theory, but is often difficult to achieve in practice. The reason is that most of us have two different voices debating with each other in our heads. Let's call the first the *Voice of Strength* and the other the *Voice of Limitation*. In any situation where we are looking to achieve peak performance, we need to increase the volume of the first voice and decrease the volume of the second voice.

Activity 20 – Amplifying my Voice of Strength

In this activity, we will examine some of the messages we are typically given by the *Voice of Limitation* and how we change these into more positive *scripts* or messages to help pave the way for future success.

In the left hand side of the table, identify up to 5 messages you regularly hear from your *Voice of Limitation*. Examples could be:

"I can never present to large groups in a confident, effective way"

"I can never seem to get enough time to do all my work"

"I can never influence my boss to understand my point of view"

Now, on the right hand side of the table, look at changing this *script* or message by thinking about concrete and positive actions you can take with reference to your Strengthscope™ results and past successes. These changed scripts represent your *Voice of Strength*.

For example:

"I can use my relationship building strength to test my presentation out on several close colleagues before I deliver it next time."

"I can ask Jane, our team administrator, for help with my efficiency weakness to ensure I plan my work better and don't feel overwhelmed."

"I can use a similar approach to influence my manager that I used last month for the budget approvals process when I presented compelling industry data to him on new server installation costs."

Voice of Limitation	Voice of Strength
I can never...	I can...
I can never...	I can...
I can never...	I can...
I can never...	I can...
I can never...	I can...

TOP TIP

Remain positive. Choosing to smile and remain upbeat, even in the face of adversity, is contagious and will help you (and those around you) feel more positively energised. This will in turn reinforce your confidence, resilience and resourcefulness, helping help you perform even better.

CHAPTER 4.2 – CELEBRATE SUCCESSES

Peak performers celebrate what's going well in a way that is meaningful for them. There are a number of benefits to celebrating success, no matter how big or small the achievement:

- By celebrating, you acknowledge that something positive has happened.

- Celebration creates positive energy and can spark creativity. All work and no play is no fun. Taking a break to celebrate raises positive feelings and creates opportunities for reflection about what works. The rewards that success brings might be just what you need to *jump start* you back into action.

- It's difficult to expect others to be aware of our strengths and successes if we don't talk about them ourselves. If we do start to tell others about what has gone well, it helps to feed the *cycle of success*.

- It's easier to remember your accomplishments and learn from them if you mark them with celebrations. Taking the time to enjoy your achievements will make it easier for you to recollect them when it comes time to list what you've done (e.g. at appraisal time or in job/promotion interviews).

Simple Ways to Celebrate Success

Perhaps you haven't been celebrating your successes because you think that a celebration involves too much time or effort. Although sometimes a major success does call for an all-out celebration, most of the time celebrations can be something simple and easy.

Here are four simple success celebrations that you can enjoy:

- **Tell someone.** Often, just telling one of your colleagues or someone close to you that you've experienced a success may be enough of a celebration – particularly if the person appreciates what went into your achievement.

- **Give yourself a reward.** Many peak performers *treat themselves* when they accomplish something special. The *treat* can be a purchase of something that they've been wanting or even allowing themselves to indulge in special food or drink they rarely get.

- **Keep a record of your success.** It's a good idea to keep a record of your successes, either in a notebook/diary or as an electronic document on your computer. While you may remember what you've completed next week or next month, it might be difficult to recollect exactly what your past successes were by the end of the year.

- **Build in some *Me Time*.** Do something you really enjoy like getting outdoors for some exercise, having a pampering day or just relaxing watching your favourite programme on TV.

Of course, celebrating success doesn't have to occur when you're on your own. It can be an excellent opportunity to get together with colleagues, friends, and family to mark your success.

Activity 21 – Lifting my *Trophy of Success*

Bearing in mind what you've been reading about the importance of celebrating success, in your *Trophy of Success* on the following page, identify:

1. The Top 3 career successes you believe you have achieved during the past 2 years.

2. The Top 3 career successes you would like to achieve in the coming 2 years.

3. What career success actually means to you. The best way to answer this is to think about what you would most like to achieve by the time you retire – is it financial success, gaining new knowledge/skills, having a major social impact, achieving a balanced life, a combination of these things, or something completely different?

4. Finally, answer the two questions on page 70 to help you think about how you can use your past successes to fuel future success and specific ways you can energise and encourage yourself along the way.

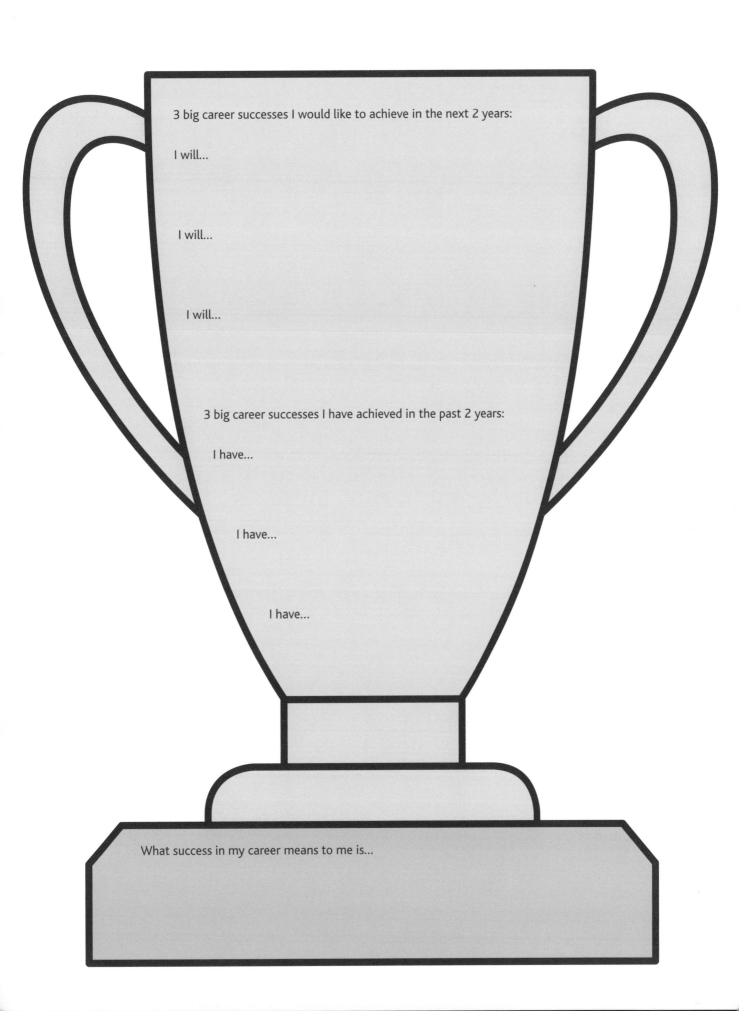

3 big career successes I would like to achieve in the next 2 years:

I will...

I will...

I will...

3 big career successes I have achieved in the past 2 years:

I have...

I have...

I have...

What success in my career means to me is...

The things I have learned from my past successes that I can use as a *springboard* for future successes are...

1.

2.

3.

Ways I would like to celebrate success that will be most energising for me going forward...

I will...

I will...

I will...

CHAPTER 4.3 – MAINTAIN MOMENTUM

While average performers often find it tough to maintain a high level of discipline and energy for self-improvement, sustained effort and repeated success, peak performers excel at building and maintaining high levels of positive energy to stay on track and reinforce a strong cycle of success.

Here are 7 powerful steps to help you to maintain momentum:

- **Reflect on what's working and why** - as you have experienced in the last activity, reflecting on what's working well and how to reinforce these productive patterns enables you to build confidence, learning and energy which becomes the fuel for future success.

- **Learning through failure and setbacks** - peak performers find learning opportunities in failures and setbacks as well as successes. They spend a lot of time and effort reviewing *moments of truth* in their performance so they can learn from these and strengthen performance problems and *gaps* that may result from limiting weaknesses, strengths in overdrive or sub-optimised strengths.

- **Invite feedback** - without high quality and focused feedback, it is difficult to determine how your strengths and performance are being perceived by your colleagues and other important people who influence your success. Inviting and listening openly to feedback from these people builds awareness of the diverse range of perspectives about your character and performance. This enables you to determine what's working well together with any changes you need to make to ensure your relationships and outcomes are continuously improved.

- **Enjoy successes, big and small** - peak performers learn to appreciate their successes, big or small. As mentioned earlier in the workbook, big successes are made up of a multitude of smaller ones so it's worthwhile taking time out to reflect on and enjoy even the smallest of improvements.

- **Share your successes** - don't complain when your performance isn't recognised by your manager, co-workers or others who influence your success. Instead, ask yourself what you have done which has resulted in you not receiving acknowledgement or credit for your contribution, as well as what you need to do differently to ensure your performance is noticed next time round.

- **Avoid being a victim** - don't allow a *victim mindset* or an attitude that you have no power over events or circumstances to drain positive energy and frustrate your performance. Take accountability for your performance and success and enjoy your freedom to find solutions and create your own future through influence and clear choices. Remember, it is largely choice, not chance, that determines your success.

- **Look for *stretch*** - peak performers are always searching for opportunities for performance stretch and future success. Challenge yourself to move outside your comfort zone. Look for opportunities to use your strengths in new, untested ways, put in place actions to improve limiting weaknesses further and apply a *Plus 10%* rule to your results, striving to achieve at least 10% more than you have achieved in the past. At the same time, ensure your stretch is realistic, taking into account your past performance as well as all the environmental factors that are likely to impact your success. Don't set overly ambitious goals as these will only demotivate you and undermine your confidence if you fall short and attract too much negative performance feedback.

TOP TIP

Find ways to remind yourself of your achievements. Successful sportspeople and sports teams keep trophy cabinets to remind them of when they were at their most successful. By recounting and replaying these successful moments in our careers, we increase our chances of future success by placing a greater focus on the positive and preparing ourselves mentally for more moments of success.

SUMMARY: SECTION 4 – ACHIEVEMENT

1. Peak performers don't only focus on learning from mistakes and shortfalls. They also look for what's working well and find meaningful ways to recognise and celebrate their strengths and achievements.

2. Having a clear understanding of and belief in your strengths enables you to build a positive self-image which raises your expectations about what you can achieve and improves your chances of success. This powerful Cycle of Success fuels future success and encourages continuous growth and improvement.

3. By celebrating what's going well for you (whether big or small), in ways that are meaningful and in line with your personality, you can create more positive energy and confidence for future successes, make your successes visible to others and ensure you are able to recall past successes.

4. Simply taking incremental steps towards change and performance improvement is insufficient to ensure success and lasting improvement. You will need to maintain high levels of positive energy to stay on track and reinforce a strong cycle of success over weeks, months and years. Steps you can take to do this include ensuring you maintain an accountable, solutions-focused attitude, learning from successes and failures, inviting feedback and looking for realistic *stretch*.

My Strengths Plan

My key learning points from this section, the most important things I need to work on are:

Further reading and references

- Dweck, C. S. (2008) *Mindset: The New Psychology of Success. New York:* Random House.